Advance praise for
"The Sipping Point: A Crash Course in Wine"

"An entertaining and educational journey through the essentials of wine. Before departing on your next wine tour, consider *The Sipping Point* required reading."

~ Pascale Bernasse, Owner French Wine Explorers

"Wine is one of life's simple and most delightful pleasures. In a simple and most delightful way, Laurie Forster's *The Sipping Point* makes that pleasure accessible to you."

~ Michael J. Gelb author of "How to Think Like Leonardo Da Vinci" and "Wine-Tasting as Team-Building"

"*The Sipping Point* is the wine mentor I always wished I had when I was learning about wine. Smart, wise, and to-the-point, Laurie Forster's book holds the answers that anyone, even someone who has loved wine for years, can use to better enjoy the nectar of the gods. Thank you for writing it, Laurie."

~ Rob Berkley, Executive Coach, co-author "Speaking of Success" with Stephen Covey and Brian Tracy and Co-creator of visionday.com

"Want wine? Get all your most pressing points addressed—even those you were afraid to ask in this invaluable resource for experts and novices alike. You'll be able to order, taste and sip wine like a pro after imbibing Laurie's practical and entertaining tips. Cheers!"

~ Susan Harrow, author of "Sell Yourself Without Selling Your Soul"

"I love wine and really knew nothing about it for years. Laurie taught me the simple and complex theories of wine and helped me enjoy drinking it on a deep and satisfying level. I have taken wine courses before but Laurie's approach is unique and empowering. Her enthusiasm and excitement are contagious and I am no longer intimidated by wine."

~ Holly Getty, Fabric Director for Calvin Klein
and Personal Style Consultant

The Sipping Point

A Crash Course in Wine

Keep on Sipping!

Laurie

The Sipping Point

A Crash Course in Wine

by Laurie Forster
The Wine Coach®

TWC Press
PO Box 763
Easton, MD 21601
(410) 820-4212

First Edition: April 2008

Publisher's Cataloging-in-Publication Data
Forster, Laurie.
      The Sipping Point: A Crash Course in Wine/
      Laurie Forster—1st ed.—Easton, MD: TWC Press, 2008 p. cm.

ISBN 13: 978-0-9817308-0-6 (paperback)
ISBN 10: 0-9817308-0-9

      1.   Wine and winemaking. I. Title

Cover and interior design by Van-garde Imagery, Inc.
Photo credits for pgs. xiii, xv, 15, 25, 29, 47, 51, 79 © Giacomo Giargia
Photo credits for back cover, p.120 and p. 124 © Paragon Light Photography

TWC Press books are available with special quantity discounts to use as premiums and sales promotions, or for use in corporate training programs. To inquire about this contact TWC Press at PO Box 763, Easton, MD 21601 or call 410-820-4212.

This book is printed in The United States of America

Acknowledgements

As I sit here trying to think of all the people who have helped me deliver this book to your hands I am humbled by all the wonderful support that I received. Most importantly I want to thank my husband, Michael, who acted as research assistant, proofreader, design consultant, consulting chef and kept things running at home while I was locked in my office finishing this book.

I also want to thank my five year old daughter, Michaela, for being so understanding for all the nights when I had to work and couldn't play.

I thank my mother, Jeanne, who is always my biggest cheerleader and showed me that with hard work anything is possible. To all the many family members and friends that had to endure hours of discussions on all things wine, selection of a title for the book and many other excruciating details, to you I raise a glass in thanks.

I cannot forget to thank my "success team" who helped in many different ways to make "The Sipping Point" something I am immensely proud of: Shannon McCaffery, Debbie Phillips, Valerie Campbell, Dorothy Fuchs, Holly Getty, Laura Schneider, Cynthia Polansky and Jamie Foster.

A special thanks to Jim Bernau for writing an amazing foreword, Heather Estay for helping me perfect my voice, Sarah Glorian for her tireless editing, and Van-garde Imagery (Dan and Darlene) for making everything look beautiful.

One last note of gratitude goes to Julia Flynn-Siler, Susan Harrow, Lisa Earle McLeod, Michael Gelb, Holly Getty, Pascale Bernasse and Rob Berkley for taking time out of their busy schedules to read and endorse my book.

Table of Contents

Foreword

How did you feel when your dinner guests asked you to make the best wine selection for the table?

Wine can be a little intimidating. Even the best of us have difficulty selecting the right German Riesling for the meal off the wine list.

Laurie Forster's "The Sipping Point" prepares you to make that wine recommendation with confidence. Wine is one of the best social mediums; it is the WD 40 of good dinner conversation and gives us something fun with which to start the conversation.

From her first awkward experience of ordering off the restaurant wine list years ago for clients, Laurie has become one the nation's foremost wine educators through her business, The Wine Coach®.

Books about wine often seem to be written in their own language (and with too many words!) discouraging many from learning the basics of enjoying wine. From selecting the right wine, opening the bottle, testing and properly serving the wine, this book gives you all the fundamentals.

I have come to know and respect Laurie through her writing, radio show and public speaking about wine. Friendship followed over glasses of wine.

Wine can become a passion - these pages may start something in you! First learning about Pinot Noir from Burgundy has resulted in acres of gorgeous vines out my front window and hundreds of French oak barrels full of delicious Oregon Pinot Noir in my cellar.

Pour yourself a glass and sit down for just a little while to enjoy this delightful easy read. Here's to great meals and friendships ahead,

Cheers!

Jim Bernau, Founder Willamette Valley Vineyards located in Salem, Oregon

About Jim Bernau:

Jim founded Willamette Valley Vineyards 25 years ago becoming one of the early pioneers in growing Pinot Noir in Oregon. His wines have achieved among the highest recognition, including being named among the "Top 100 Wines in the World" by Wine Spectator magazine. Jim has received the Outstanding Service Award as a result of his leadership of the Oregon Winegrowers Association as President and the Founders Award for his role in establishing the Oregon Wine Board. He was recently presented the Founders Award from the state's leading organization for sustainable practice for his advocacy of environmentally responsible vineyard and winemaking practices.

Preface

A few words of wisdom from The Wine Coach®

In my past life, I worked as a sales executive for an internet software company, traveling all over the country and working with some of the finest minds in the software business. One of the aspects of my job that I enjoyed most was entertaining prospective clients, which typically meant taking them out to dinner to share great food and wine.

My love of wine was not immediate but rather grew over time. One reason was that like most other kids in suburban households in America, I did not grow up enjoying or learning about wine at the dinner table. In fact as a child of the eighties, I had more exposure to wine coolers and wine in a box than wine in a bottle!

I'll never forget the first time I was handed an extensive wine list. Everyone at the table looked to me to choose the perfect wine selection to accompany our meal. In a panic, I quickly scanned the list for anything familiar and hoped my client couldn't see how nervous I was. On other occasions, I tried asking the waiter for help. But often my request was greeted with indifference, or worse yet, an attitude of snobbish disdain for my ignorance. Those experiences motivated me to study wine so I could navigate a wine list and dazzle my clients unassisted!

Today, wine is both my passion and my career. I have made it my mission to save you from those uncomfortable, awkward moments I experienced. This guide is meant to arm you with the essential things you need to know about wine. It is a quick reference guide that you will be able to refer to over and over again. And hopefully, it will inspire you to go deeper into the study and enjoyment of wines!

As The Wine Coach®, my goal is to help everyone connect with wine in a way that is approachable and fun. Unlike many other wine books, this one is written in plain English. I have tried to take out the jargon and make these wine tips user-friendly. This guide includes many of the shortcuts, secrets and analogies I learned during my sommelier training.

I urge you to share this with your fellow wine lovers and perhaps form a wine club. You'll find that not only will you learn more about wine but you will learn more about each other as well. The old proverb is true: "Over a bottle of wine many a friend is made."

Cheers,
Laurie Forster, The Wine Coach®

"What is the best way to learn about wine? Forget about textbooks and ratings—just pull that cork!"

~ Laurie Forster, The Wine Coach®

Coming Uncorked

Most fundamental to enjoying good wine is getting the bottle open! It's actually harder to explain than to do, but here are some key tips to doing this with a traditional waiter's corkscrew without breaking a sweat.

Remove the capsule. To remove the metal foil or "capsule" that covers the wine bottle's neck, pull out the small knife in the cork screw housing. Holding your index finger on the back of the knife, press firmly under the lower lip or bevel at the top of the bottle. Cutting under the lower lip will ensure that the foil does not come in contact with the wine while pouring. Keep your thumb on the opposite side as a guide and to make sure you do not cut yourself. Rotate the knife around the bottle to cut the capsule completely. Remember to rotate the knife, not the bottle, while cutting the capsule to avoid agitating the wine. *Caution:* capsules can have sharp edges.

Quick Tip: If you are in a hurry you can do one of two things. Buy a foil cutter that makes this process effortless or use this shortcut. To open a bottle in a casual setting, you can shimmy off the foil by twisting the entire capsule back and forth while pulling up. This will only work with the aluminum covering not plastic and is only recommended in a wine emergency!

Screw loose. Holding the bottle steady, center the point of the spiral corkscrew (sometimes called the "worm") on the cork and insert. Holding the corkscrew upright, not angled, twist the corkscrew (not the bottle) until it is almost all the way into the cork.

 **Leverage your assets.** Place the lever of the corkscrew on top of the lip of the bottle. Holding the lever in place with your thumb, apply pressure on the corkscrew handle and ease the cork almost completely out. Then grab the cork with your hand and rock the cork to slowly release it—this avoids the rude burp of the cork! Check the cork to ensure that it is moist on the end indicating that the bottle was stored properly on its side.

Do's & don'ts. It's okay to rest the bottle on a corner of the table, or if the wine is white or sparkling, in an ice bucket as you open it. ***Do not use your body as leverage or put it between your legs to pull out the cork***—too tacky!

Broken cork? Place the worm back into the bottle on top of the broken cork, angling it to the outside of the neck; twist it in and lever it out as above. Remove bits of cork by straining through a metal tea strainer.

Do the twist. If your wine has a screw cap rather than a traditional cork, do not think this means your wine is inferior! Many wineries are now using screw caps to prevent wines from being "corked." There is a compound called TCA or trichloroanisole (if you like big words) that infects corks and ruins the wine. A wine that is corked often smells like a musty basement. To properly open a screw cap wine, grab the bottom part of the metal capsule or the neck and give a firm twist— the cap will come off effortlessly.

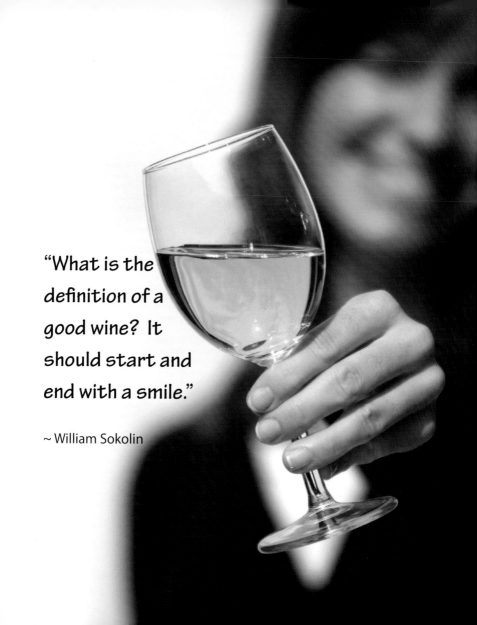

"What is the definition of a good wine? It should start and end with a smile."

~ William Sokolin

Taste Test

To fully appreciate wine, you should use all of your senses, relax and enjoy! There are no absolute rules to tasting wine, these steps are general guidelines.

Use your brain. As you move through each step of wine tasting, describe what you see, smell, and taste. You don't need to know wine terminology. Just use words that come to mind—describe your impressions to enhance the experience.

Give it the eye. Pour a glass of wine and observe its color, clarity, and brilliance. The best way to view a wine is to hold it at a 45 degree angle against a white background, such as a white piece of paper or tablecloth. Note the intensity of color, presence of sediment or fading of color at the rim. Wine should not be cloudy or hazy. If this is the case it could indicate a problem with the wine. Take your time and appreciate it from all angles.

Take a whiff. To get a good impression of your wine's aroma take a quick whiff to gain a first impression. Then gently swirl your glass to enhance the wine's natural aromas.

Poke your nose in. Really! Stick your nose deep into the glass and inhale through your nose. Gently swirl the wine to let the aromas mix and mingle, and sniff again. Aromas of our favorite fruits, flowers or foods are perceived by our nose not our tongue. Smelling is 80% of the tasting process, so don't short change this step. Think of your nose as your best asset in the tasting process

Taste in stages. Take a sip and let it roll around on your tongue. Next, let a small breath of air in and allow the wine and air to mingle. This allows you to taste the flavors more fully. The main role of our tongues is to perceive sweet, sour, salty or bitter characteristics of the wine. The sour or pucker factor you may feel is the wine's acidity. Some red wines have a bitter or astringent sensation that are called tannins, which come from grape skins and will sometimes feel like your mouth is dry.

Swallow & savor! The "finish" is the taste and sensation that lingers after you swallow. Rather than another gulp, see what your wine offers in between sips. A wine that you continue to taste for some time after swallowing would be described as having a long finish. Many wines are not truly their best until paired with the right dish— so don't forget to try them with food.

Record for posterity. Record your thoughts and impressions. If you really enjoyed the wine, jot down information from the label. (Or if it was not enjoyable, note that too!).

For a useful format to record your wine notes see page 119, to download *visit:* www.thewinecoach.com/thesippingpoint

"The primary purpose of wine is
to make food taste better."

~ Myra Waldo

Matchmaking: Food & Wine

Matching foods and wines is like a dance. It can be complex, but a few basic tips and your own taste buds will guide you best. Gather some friends, wines and food and test these tips yourself!

Bodyweight. Like milk—skim, whole and cream—wines can be distinguished by weight: light-bodied, medium-bodied and full-bodied. Higher alcohol content usually means a fuller bodied wine. As a general rule, light-bodied wines are 7-11%, medium run between 11-13%, and full-bodied are over 13%.

Weight class. Pair heavier foods with heavier wines, lighter fare with lighter wines. This is pretty intuitive. For instance, a crisp summer seafood salad would be overwhelmed by a hearty Cabernet. A light, fruity Pinot Grigio would be lost paired with a New York strip steak.

Salt & acid. Salt lowers your perception of the acid, which is that tangy, sharp sensation in wine. Salty foods need wines with higher acid, like Sauvignon Blanc or Pinot Noir, rather than their less-acidic counterparts, Chardonnay or Shiraz (Syrah).

Acid to acid. Matching high acid wines with high acid foods works like a double negative—they neutralize each other. Think Sauvignon Blanc and goat cheese, separately, each is quite acidic, but together they are heavenly.

Sugar 'n spice. Sweet foods, like desserts, need a wine that is one degree sweeter. If the wine is drier or equal in sweetness, it will lose much of its taste. Sweet wines tone down spicy foods, whereas high alcohol, dry wines intensify the heat or spice.

Smoky with oaky. Foods that are grilled or have smoky flavors will match nicely with wines that have a sense of oakiness. Think grilled fish with an oaky California Chardonnay or a grilled steak with a hearty California Cabernet.

A wine sandwich. Want a sure fire method to evaluate whether a wine and food combination works? Make a wine sandwich. Take a sip of the wine, then a bite of your food and then a second sip of your wine. Wine, food, wine—that's the sandwich! The second sip of your wine will show how the food alters the wine, ideally for the better!

Food For Thought

✔ Drink wine, and you will sleep well. Sleep well and you will not sin. Avoid sin, and you will be saved. Ergo, drink wine and be saved.

✔ Old wine and old friends are enough provision.

✔ With wine and hope, anything is possible.

✔ In water one sees one's own face, but in wine one beholds the heart of another.

✔ There are more old wine drinkers than old doctors.

Wine Glasses 101

There's a reason why wine isn't served in Dixie cups or beer steins! Here are wine glass basics:

Tulips, please! A good wine glass has a tulip-shaped bowl that tapers toward the top. Why? The shape keeps aromas in the glass, enhancing your tasting enjoyment.

Crystal or glass? Real crystal has a rough surface that helps agitate wine as we swirl which releases aromas that add to taste. It also encourages the effervescence of Champagnes and sparkling wines.

Colored or plain? It's hard to enjoy the beautiful, true colors of wine through glass that is etched, colored, or heavily decorated. Less is more, and clear is excellent!

Which glass for which wine? Wines are served in different glasses to enhance their flavor, not just to confuse you! White wine glasses are smaller and narrower to allow the delicate aromas of these wines to be concentrated in the glass. The broad bowls of red wine glasses provide more swirling surface, allowing oxygen to unlock their flavors.

The bubbles of sparking wines and Champagnes will sparkle more in slender flute-shaped glasses.

On a shoestring budget? Buy good all-purpose crystal wine glasses that are tulip-shaped and about 8-10 inches tall (or ask Santa for a great set next Christmas!).

Stemless glasses? Perhaps not the connoisseur's choice, but stemless glasses are great for large, casual parties and are dishwasher safe. Since most wine glasses break at the stem, these glasses will cut down on your stemware budget. An added bonus—stemless glasses are easier to hold for those with arthritic hands.

Handling a Wine Glass

There are practical reasons, not snobbery, behind proper ways to hold a wineglass.

Mitts off. A wine glass is held at the stem and *not* at the bowl for a couple of reasons. First, you don't want your hands to warm the wine (unless it has been served too cold and needs warming). Second, no matter how tidy you are, your fingers will leave prints and mar the beauty of the wine as seen through the glass.

Balancing act. Most people hold the glass stem in the middle for better balance and use some combination of thumb on one side creating pressure against fingers on the other side. Some folks opt for the bottom of the glass. Figure out what seems the most stable and natural to you.

At rest. When you put your wine glass down on a coffee table or side table, it should be on a coaster (this is even more important for the wine bottle itself which might drip). Coasters usually aren't necessary on a dining table for glasses.

The set up. At a restaurant or a friend's dinner table, the wine glasses placed to the right of the plate are yours. Depending on the meal, you may have full selection of wine glasses. In order left to right (see diagram below), the glasses will be arranged as follows: water glass-E (above the knife), red wine-F, white wine-G. Sometimes the red wine glass is placed above the water and white wine glasses to form a triangle. Dessert glasses are usually brought out later. In a restaurant, unnecessary glasses will usually be removed once you've made your selection.

Crystal Clear

Caring for your wine glasses: Crystal is more porous than glass, bringing out the flavor and visual beauty of wine—but they will need a little TLC and technique in cleaning.

Think hot! Rinse your wine glasses in the hottest water you can stand.

No soap! Dish soap leaves a residue that affects taste and aroma. Who needs Eau de Palmolive? If you must use soap, use it sparingly and rinse thoroughly. Ivory Soap (not detergent) will leave less residue.

Let 'em drain. Set your glasses upside down in a drain rack or on a linen towel. If drying with a towel, use linen (less lint and better shine) and take care not to shove too much towel into the bowl of the glass to avoid breakage.

Dishwasher safe? Probably not. But if you must use the dishwasher, make sure glasses can't rattle around and get chipped. Take them out before the dry cycle.

Looking cloudy? Water spots? Cabernet stains? Fill glasses with water and plop in some "Efferdent" (sans dentures, please!). You can also try baking soda and water.

Residual taste? Heavily chlorinated water or detergent may leave a residual flavor. Try rinsing glasses with a splash of vodka in rinse water. Or, right before serving, splash a touch of the wine you're pouring, swirl in the glass and dump it out. This is commonplace in Italy and they call it "preparing the glasses."

Steam for extra shine! Hold your glasses upside down over steaming water and then polish with a linen tea towel. This is the secret trick caterers use to make glasses sparkle.

"A bottle of wine contains more philosophy than all the books in the world"

~ Louis Pasteur

Wine Serving Temps

Different wines are best served at different temperatures. Here are some rules of thumb with the logic behind them:

Why chill whites? White wines are ideally served at 45-50°F. The aromas/flavors intensify as the wine warms. Chilling reduces the perception of acid in crisp wines, bolsters whites with less acid, and makes it more refreshing! Champagne and sparkling wines should be served a bit cooler around 40-45°F.

Reds at room temp? This was true before central heating, when house temperatures ran 50-65°F. Today, "room temperature" is often considerably warmer. Red wines should be served at 60-65°F. If served cooler, tannins or bitter flavors are accentuated. Soft reds low in tannins can handle a lower temperature.

Getting it right. Refrigerators are set at about 35-39°F. Wine temperature will lower about 4 degrees every 10 minutes, and will warm at the same rate. So, remove a fully chilled white wine from the refrigerator about 10 to 15 minutes before serving. Conversely, a "room temperature" red can be chilled for 10-20 minutes to bring it to its optimal temperature of 60-65°F.

What if it's wrong? The next time you're out to dinner, "take the temperature" of the bottle that a waiter presents to you. It should feel slightly cool. If it's too warm, don't hesitate to ask that your wine be put on ice for a few minutes (even if it is a red).

Getting specific: Full-bodied reds (Cabernet, Sauvignon, Merlot, Zinfandel, Shiraz/Syrah): 60-65°F; lighter bodied reds (Beaujolais, Pinot Noir, Chianti, Rosé) and full-bodied whites, (Chardonnay, Viognier): 50-60°F; lighter whites (dry Riesling, Sauvignon Blanc, Chenin Blanc), Ice Wine and Vintage Champagne: 45-50°F; Champagne and Sparkling Wines: 40-45°F; Dessert Wines (Sauternes or late harvest wines): 50-60°F.

All locked up. A white wine served too cold will have its flavors locked up. As it warms, the flavors will develop. If you are forced to choke down a lesser quality wine, drink it ice cold. All you will notice is that it is cool and refreshing, not unpleasant!

"Wine is sunlight,
held together
by water."

~Galileo

Half Empty, Half Full

Preserving Leftover Wine: It's unclear why you would ever have leftovers of a great wine, but in the unlikely event that you do . . .

Know your enemy: Air! Bacteria in the air will turn an open bottle of wine to vinegar. The air itself will oxidize wine, dulling its taste.

Just chill! Whether white or red, chilling leftover wine can slow the deterioration. Take red out of the refrigerator an hour or so before pouring to bring back to room temperature.

Shrink the bottle. Many great wines are made in half-bottle sizes (375 ml) that have approximately 2.5 glasses in them. One option, if you live alone, is to purchase these in lieu of the larger bottles. You can also use them to preserve wine by pouring your leftover wine (carefully, so as to avoid aerating it) into a clean half-bottle that you keep on hand for just such an occasion. A smaller bottle means there is less air to break down your wine.

Suck it out! Clients of mine swear by vacuum preservers (rubber stoppers that come with a pump that sucks the air out of your wine bottle) or aerosol products which use argon to displace air in your bottle.

No spin the bottle! If wine is decanted then poured back into its original bottle, more air will be dissolved within the wine. Shaking and swirling the wine unnecessarily will also infuse more air. So, handle leftover wine as little as possible to limit exposure to air.

How long have you got? Most folks agree that an opened bottle of wine, treated tenderly, will have up to three days to live. (Of course, if it tastes good to you on day five, drink up!). You can also use leftover wine for cooking or to make vinegar.

"Wine improves with age.
The older I get, the better I like it."

~ Anonymous

Wine TLC

Wine is a living thing that requires proper care and nurturing to grow and develop as the winemaker intended. Some tips:

Roadtrip. Get your wine home ASAP! Temperature fluctuations in a car, combined with extra vibrations from driving, may cause wine to age prematurely—and taste lousy.

Avoid the chill. Do NOT store wine in a refrigerator unless it will be consumed within a few days. Most refrigerators constantly vibrate and maintain temperatures around 35-39°F with low humidity—not ideal conditions for wine. Smells in the refrigerator can also permeate the cork.

Cool & even! Optimal temperature for wine storage is 52-57°F. Avoiding fluctuations of temperature is the most important thing so if you have a space that is consistently 60°F, that's great!

Bad vibes. Vibrations from transportation or improper storage will disrupt the flavor compounds, stir up sediment and interfere with proper aging.

Sideways. Wine is stored on its side to keep the cork moist. Dry corks will crack or shrink, allowing unwanted air to leak in. It is also necessary to maintain a humidity level of about 70-75% where the wine is stored so the corks will not dry out.

Light sensitive. Keep wine away from direct sunlight or bright light. Modern bottles have good UV filters, but light still penetrates, making wine "light struck" causing an unpleasant aroma. Choose incandescent bulbs in your wine storage area over fluorescents.

Know when to drink it. Generally, more expensive wines are meant to be aged longer and red wines last longer than white. Most of the wines we purchase for every day use will not improve with age. Drink up before it's past its prime!

Ordering Wine for Your Table

Sharing a bottle of wine should be fun, not a nerve wracking détente negotiation! Some tips to make it easy:

A stall tactic. Buy yourself a little time by ordering a sparkling or white wine for everyone to start. It will go well with most salads and appetizers, giving you a chance to study the wine list.

Take a poll. Find out what everyone will order for their main course. Ask those in your party for their specific preferences ("What do you normally enjoy, red or white?"). Feel free to ignore suggestions that don't work for the whole group.

Play it safe. Choose one or two all-purpose wines. For whites, try ordering a dry white Riesling, Sauvignon Blanc or Pinot Grigio (Pinot Gris); for reds, Pinot Noir, Sangiovese or Barbera are all great choices. All of these are versatile, with enough fruit and enough acid to stand up to all types of foods including salty, acidic, and spicy foods.

Cachet over cash. You don't have to spend mega-bucks to find a pleasing wine for your guests. Wines priced in the mid to high end are often a better value because they are not marked up as much as low end wines. Ordering a high-priced wine you have not tasted can be risky. Restaurants are not the place to experiment considering that wines are marked up 2-3 times their wholesale cost. The best strategy is to figure out your price range of wines with which you are familiar and opting for the higher end of that range to get the best value.

You've got a friend. Team up with the sommelier or your knowledgeable waiter. These people are usually wine lovers too, but they don't have Donald Trump budgets! They'll know the best values on their list. A tip: With the sommelier over your shoulder, point to the price of the wine and say, "This is a wine I'm considering, what would you suggest?" Without your guests being aware, this will let your sommelier know your price range.

Be understood. Let's face it, most of us are not experts in French, Spanish or Italian. That doesn't stop us from enjoying the wine, right? If you find a great wine you want to order, but are afraid to pronounce it, look for the Bin Number listed to the left of the wine. Many restaurants use these as a method to organize their wine inventory. If the list doesn't show bin numbers, point to the wine in question and any astute server will get the message.

Do your homework. If you are dining out for a special occasion like an anniversary, birthday or to close a big deal and you want to impress your guests—consider visiting the restaurant's website to view their wine list ahead of time. If it is not listed online you can ask for it to be faxed to you ahead of time. Asking for their assistance in pre-selecting a wine can be a good idea as well.

B.Y.O.B. In some states you are allowed to bring a bottle of your own wine to a restaurant. In the case where the restaurant does not already serve wine, they will be happy to help you open, serve and chill your wine without a fee.

If you bring your bottle to an establishment that already sells wine, they will most likely charge you a "corkage fee." The corkage fee covers the service of your wine and some of the revenue lost. If you choose to do this where they already have a list, I suggest that you order another bottle off their list as a courtesy. Maybe a half bottle of sparkling wine to begin or a dessert wine at the end. Typically you want to avoid bringing wines that are on their wine list already or inexpensive table wines. This corkage fee is usually expected to be for a guest bringing a special bottle.

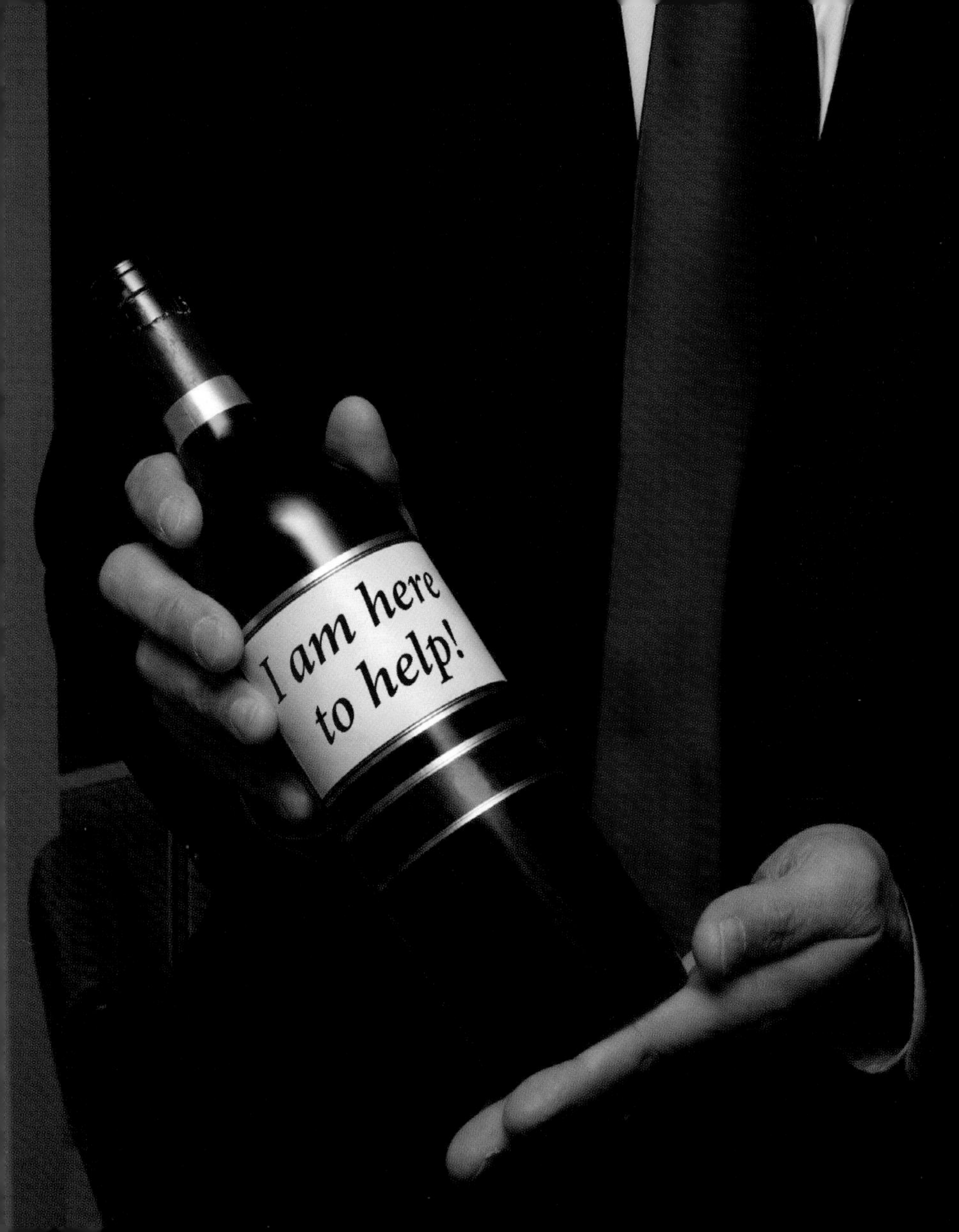
I am here
to help!

How to Use the Sommelier

Sommeliers are wine lovers just like you, but they know a heck of a lot more! Leverage that knowledge to discover great wines!

Who is this guy (or gal)? A sommelier (pronounced so-mel-YAY) has specific training in wine and is the one who trains the wait staff, orders the wine, and creates the wine list in fine dining restaurants. Not all restaurants have sommeliers, but any that have an extensive wine list should have people on staff who are knowledgeable about their wines.

Choices, choices. It's the sommelier's job to help diners choose wines. Use them as you would any professional consultant. Give them information (what food you're ordering, your preferences) and tip them off to your budget by *pointing to the price* of a wine you're considering. Let them know if you want to experiment or stick with something safe.

Ask and ye shall receive. Good questions will get good responses: "What are you most excited about?" or "What do you think is the best value on the list?" Listen and learn! If you are dealing with a waiter who doesn't seem to know the wine list, ask (nicely) if there is someone more knowledgeable to consult.

The inside scoop. Most sommeliers are eager to help and have tasted most (if not all) of the wines on their list. Those of us who have chosen wine as a career enjoy drinking wine every night, but don't necessarily have large budgets. Sommeliers and servers will know the best bargains, because that is likely what they are drinking at home!

Pouring it on. Your waiter or sommelier should pour the entire bottle of wine through the evening. You should not run empty for long or have to pour your own (though many of us do in casual restaurant settings!).

A tip for their tips? A sommelier gets a percentage of wine sales so you don't need to tip them separately. However, a nice compliment about their expertise or service will be appreciated!

The Restaurant Ritual

Ordering a bottle of wine in a restaurant is complete with traditions that perplex many wine drinkers. Here are the keys to what I call "the restaurant ritual."

The Lead Role. Let's review the roles. The person ordering the wine is considered the "host" regardless of gender. The server will present the bottle and either point to the label or verbally announce the selection. This step is to ensure they are serving the correct wine and vintage requested. Pay particular attention to this step if you ordered a vintage that was exceptional. The vintages delivered to the restaurant often change without notice and the restaurant itself may not have noticed. You may want to look for an alternate choice if you had your heart set on a specific year.

Cork Confusion. Next, the server will open the wine and place the cork to the right of the host. This step sometimes confuses the customer. What do you do with the cork? Simply put: nothing. You can examine the end to ensure it is moist. Wines stored correctly on the side will have moist corks. The cork will not tell you if the wine is bad, so smelling it is not necessary.

Nodding Off. The server will then pour a small taste in the host's wine glass to allow the host to check for flaws. The wine should be at least smelled and can be tasted as well. They are looking for a nod or comment that it is fine. Glowing compliments are not necessary! Wine with flaws will smell like a musty basement or vinegar. Don't skip this step when you order a second bottle of the same wine (1 in 10 bottles of wine are "corked" or flawed). Once you have approved the wine, the server will fill the wine glasses in a clockwise manner, ladies first with the host being last.

Drink Up. Follow these steps so next time you order a bottle of wine you can sit back and enjoy the ritual!

"Good wine ruins the purse;
bad wine ruins the stomach."

~ Spanish Saying

Where to Buy Wine?

So many options! From your local drug store to sites on the internet, where should an aspiring winer shop?

Go pro. Your best option is to find a local wine merchant and build a relationship. These folks taste 30-60 wines per week. Once they know your tastes, they can steer you to some terrific buys. Ideally, your wine merchant has regular tastings to let you try different wines. In some areas, good wine merchants can also be found at gourmet food stores.

On the net. A great way to learn about new wines is to join a wine club on the internet. Each month, you'll be sent a couple of wines to expand your repertoire. Before purchasing wines on the internet, be sure you know what you want—returning wine can be iffy and expensive. *Note:* Buying wines over the internet is not legal in all states!

On tour. It's exciting to buy wine from its very own tasting room! But don't buy wine after a long day of tasting (when too many sips have impaired your taste buds) and don't buy a "sympathy" bottle of a wine you don't like. Rather than paying for shipping or lugging it home, ask about the wine's availability in your home state. Be aware that you can no longer carry wine onto an airplane. (Do you really want that Cabernet rattling around in your suitcase in the cargo hold?)

Best bets. Ideally, you want to buy wine where it's been handled with care, i.e., stored on its side, temperature controlled, and not in direct sunlight. If conditions are not perfect, the wine will still probably be okay if the merchant sells wine in high volume, moving it off the shelf quickly.

Don't be a book worm! It is easy to fall in love with helpful wine guides that rate wines. Rather than using them as your wine bible, use them as a great starting point for ideas. Your local store will often have similar quality wines that are less expensive. Remember what you learned in economics about supply and demand: if it makes the "Top" list or is given a rating of 90 or higher, expect to pay a premium!

"The taste of a good wine
is remembered long after
the price is forgotten."

~ Anonymous

Buying Wine for Events

Finally! A good use of the math you learned in fourth grade!

Stand up & be counted. For a few hours of chatting and snacking (f.k.a. the cocktail party), assume each wine-drinking guest will consume a five-ounce glass every hour. If you've invited 20 wine-drinkers and plan a two hour party, that's five ounces per hour times two hours, so each person will drink 10 ounces. Now multiply 10 ounces by 20 guests which equals 200 ounces needed, divided by 25 (approximate number of ounces in a bottle) equals eight bottles. There are 12 bottles in a case—whew! Often wine stores offer discounts for purchasing a case or more so you may want to consider buying a few extra bottles.

Wine & dine. If serving special wines at a dinner party, you can use a similar equation. But the total will depend on the number of courses, different wines you'll serve, and the general pacing of the evening. A rough rule of thumb: one bottle per person.

Wedding wines. Wedding toasts taste better with a flute of champagne or sparkling wine. If you are serving other wines, assume at least one flute of bubbly for each guest. There are approximately 7 flutes per bottle so do the math from there (some guests will likely stick with bubbly for the entire party).

How much of which? How much white, red, or sparkling? It will vary by season. We tend toward lighter whites and sparkling wines in summer but gravitate toward reds in colder months. In general it's now estimated that 60% of people prefer red to white.

What's for dinner? Consider your menu when selecting a wine lineup. If focusing on Italian cuisine, try choosing wines from that region. Menus heavy in seafood will pair well with sparkling, white and lighter reds, whereas meatier menus will require you to pull out the big guns of full-bodied reds!

Go dutch? A great way to have a fabulous party that won't break the bank is to invite everyone to bring a bottle of wine and an appetizer. Pick a theme (Australian Shiraz, whites under $20) and have an instant wine tasting party. For more tips on creating a wine tasting party or club, read "It's no fun to drink alone" on page 113.

HORST DOHM
FLASCHENPOST AUS
PIEMONT

Die sechzig großen Weine
Fotografiert von Jürgen Röhrscheid

Keyser

"The best use of bad wine is to drive away poor relations."

~ French Proverb

Bad Wine: What to Do?

One out of every 10 bottles of wine is "corked" or otherwise compromised. Here's how to tell and what to do about it.

Is it really bad? "Bad" wine is not simply a wine you don't like; it is wine that has been compromised. If the wine's aroma is sherry-like, it may have oxidized. If it smells musty or like mildew, it might be "corked," which occurs when real corks become contaminated with a naturally occurring compound called trichloroanisole or TCA.

Out on the town. If you suspect the wine is bad while dining at a restaurant, mention it to the sommelier or waiter as soon as the wine is poured. No need to make a big deal about it. A simple, "I think there might be something wrong with the wine" will get their attention. They should return the wine immediately and bring you another bottle.

One bad, all bad? One bad bottle in a case does not mean that the entire case is bad. In a restaurant, you are probably safe to order the same wine again. At home, if you discover a bad wine don't pour the bad bottle down the drain and certainly don't drink it! Immediately re-cork it to bring it back to your wine merchant for a replacement or refund.

At a party. If the wine is truly compromised, take the host aside to tell him in private. To save embarrassment, let him know that it is not uncommon. If the wine is not technically "bad" but simply doesn't taste good, don't say a word but "misplace" your wine glass and drink beer instead!

Good taste. Remember that what you think is a great wine may not be the same as what your husband, girlfriend or brother thinks. Our taste in wine, like our taste in fashion or home décor, is very personal. Don't insult your host by expressing your opinion on their selections. Likewise, if it is your party, don't expect everyone to love every wine you chose. If you have a selection of wine styles (such as sparkling, crisp versus mellow whites, light fruity versus full-bodied dry reds, sweet wines, etc.), everyone will certainly find something they like.

Awkward Wine Moments

Wine doesn't create awkward moments but wine drinkers can. Moving gracefully through embarrassment . . .

I think you've had enough. It's embarrassing and dangerous when guests over imbibe. Avoid the situation by pacing wine, water and food. ALWAYS have food available, even at the beginning of a party. For an extended evening, pour 1-2 oz. servings (one finger = one oz.) rather than the "normal" 4-5 oz. portions. Offer your inebriated guest a ride home or a place to stay (make it a slumber party!). *Myth:* Coffee will sober them up.

Crying over spilt wine. A guest spills the Cabernet on your white sofa, or breaks one of your favorite wine glasses. Great hosts simply don't make a big deal of it! Sop up the mess and cover it with a towel or napkin. Hand your accident prone guest a new glass quickly—they'll need it! Using stemless glasses can be one way to avoid these situations.

White elephant wine. When a guest brings a wine that is inappropriate (or something you would not usually want to serve your guests),

"Wine makes a man more pleased
with himself; I do not say it makes
him more pleasing to others."

~ Samuel Johnson

don't panic! You are not required to serve it that night. Tell them how much you look forward to enjoying it later. Your guest shouldn't insist that it be opened that night. If they are insistent, save the bottle for the end of the evening when everyone's palates are a bit impaired.

Say what? When you hear someone mispronouncing a wine name or grape varietal, don't correct them in public. If they are a close friend you might catch them in a private moment and say something like "I think I have heard it said this way . . . ." Another option is to say the word again later in the evening with the correct pronunciation. Learning about wine is intimidating and we can't all be expected to say everything right the first time. A great place to visit when learning to speak the language of wine is www.stratsplace.com. They have a living wine dictionary that has live audio clips with pronunciations of over 600 wine words!

Crying over Spilled Wine

Dealing with Wine Stains: A great glass of wine spilled on the carpet is a tragedy in itself! A stain just adds insult to injury. These tips will help those pesky stains disappear.

Red vs. white. White wine spills are relatively easy, but reds have tannins and dark colors that can leave a bad stain. For unexplained reasons, red wine also has a propensity for spilling onto white carpets and garments!

Catch it quick! Your best bet is to tackle it quickly. Remove the garment or treat it while wearing it; soak up the carpet and table cloth stains while the party is in full swing.

Blot, don't mash! First step is to sop up as much liquid as you can. Blot, don't rub! Rubbing forces stains into fabric.

Whatever is on hand. There are numerous homegrown treatments that wine spillers swear by, try one or more:

- Dump salt on the stain; leave overnight and vacuum

- Pour white wine or club soda on the stain and sop it up

- Stretch stained part of garment over a bowl and pour boiling water through it

- Treat with a combination of hydrogen peroxide and dish soap or carpet shampoo (tests by UC Davis claim this beats any other method—even commercial products)

Drip dry only. Your dryer will set the stain further so make sure the stain is gone before you throw your garment in.

Don't give up! Patience and creativity—application of these methods will eventually triumph over that stain. If not, consider it a wonderful reminder of the fun you had!

Shout it out. There are a myriad of products on the market that are created just to remove red wine stains. You will find products like Wine Away at your local wine store or online wine store.

The Dreaded Hangover

Most wine lovers have at times experienced this morning-after result of a night of enjoying wine. Here are some tips if you do, and preventative measures so you don't!

Water to wine. Too much of a good thing is not the only cause of morning-after headaches. Another culprit is dehydration. To avoid this fate, drink at least as much water as wine during the evening and drink a big glass of water before bed.

Congeners and other pesky things. Congeners, like tannins and histamines, are natural by-products of alcohol fermentation. The higher the congener content in your drink, the greater the hangover you can expect. Gin and vodka have the fewest congeners, bourbon and red wine have the most. Red wines contain a higher concentration of histamines than whites so if they give you a headache, try an antihistamine or switch to white. Some people are sensitive to the tannins found in red wines, chocolate and tea. Tannins can also intensify the dehydrating effects of wine.

Sulfites to blame? Sulfites have been used safely to preserve wine throughout history. People who are sensitive to sulfites will have trouble breathing, which is a much bigger problem than a headache! If you know you are allergic to sulfites, try organic wines that are lower in sulfites. Sulfites naturally occur in wine, so it is difficult to find a wine that will have no sulfites.

Slow down! Not only will you enjoy the wine more, but your kidney can only handle 3-4 oz. per hour. So sip, don't gulp, and pace yourself.

Gnosh along. Eating while drinking can slow down the absorption of alcohol. Milk can also help line the stomach.

Gender bias. Women process alcohol slower than men due to their higher percentage of body fat, lower body weight and lower levels of the enzyme dehydrogenase, which works to break down alcohol. So keeping pace with the guys actually makes females more intoxicated—and more prone to a hangover.

"A hangover is when you open
your eyes and wish you hadn't."

~ Anonymous

"Too much of anything is bad, but too much Champagne is just right"

~ Mark Twain

Uncorking the Bubbly

Mom wasn't kidding when she warned that you can pop an eye out with champagne. Though that POP can be fun, you'll sacrifice too much bubbly. Save the excitement for the toast!

Steady eddy. Unless you're going for a record for long-distance cork flight, DO NOT shake the bottle before opening! And make sure it's chilled—if it's warm, its can be volatile!

Heavy metal. Peel or cut off the top of the foil covering. Be careful since the foil sometimes has sharp edges.

Are you wired? Point the bottle at a 45 degree angle in a safe direction, i.e., away from family, friends and valued breakables! Grab a clean towel and place it between your hand and the cork while untwisting the wire cage that covers the cork. It is safest to loosen but leave the cage on while opening. Do not remove the cage totally unless you are ready for an explosion!

Twist, don't shout. With one hand over the cork and cage, SLOWLY turn the bottle with the other hand. You should feel the cork loosen slightly. Keep pushing downward on the cork as it loosens and finally releases. You'll hear a slight whoosh of pressure releasing. It has been said that the perfect opening of Champagne makes no more noise than a contented woman. Of course, that may depend on the woman, right?

A one & a two. Be patient! Wait a few seconds for the wine to settle before fully removing the cork with your upper hand. Have your towel ready to catch any overly enthusiastic bubbles that escape.

Check it out. Take a small taste of the bubbly to ensure that it is not corked. Just like still wines, sparkling wine corks can get infected and compromise that taste of the wine. If it smells or tastes musty, you may want to start over!

Easy does it. Pour the champagne SLOWLY and gently to avoid creating a head that foams over. Crystal flutes (not chilled, thank you!) will allow your bubbly to be its bubbliest!

Know Your Champagne

This quote says it all: "In victory, you deserve Champagne, in defeat, you need it." ~Napoleon (of course). Officially the only wines from the Champagne region of France are allowed to use the term Champagne. Here is what makes them so special.

A great team. There are three grapes that are used in Champagne: Chardonnay, Pinot Noir, and Pinot Meunier (pronounced Pee-Noh Moon-yay). The latter are red grapes, and former is white. Most Champagne is made by blending these three grapes to take advantage of each grape's varietal character. It is said that Chardonnay adds elegance; Pinot Noir power; and Pinot Meunier fruitiness.

Special sparklers. Champagnes that bear the term *Blanc de Blancs* (translated "white from whites") are made entirely from the Chardonnay grape and tend to be more elegant and less fruity. In contrast, sparklers that bear the term *Blanc de Noirs* (translated "white from blacks") use only the red grapes—Pinot Noir and Pinot Meunier, making them more fruity and powerful.

How sweet it is. Champagne, as well as most sparkling wines, are made in a variety of styles, listed from driest to sweetest, include: Extra (or Ultra) Brut, Brut, Extra Dry, Sec, Demi-sec, and Doux.

In the house. NV stands for Non Vintage and means the wine is a blend of various harvests and intended to be an expression of a particular winery's style referred to as a "house style." This way they can ensure that every time you sip Krug or Veuve Clicquot Non Vintage, for instance, it will taste the same.

What a year! If the growing season is excellent, some Champagne or sparkling wine producers will create a vintage sparkler that lists the year of harvest on the bottle. These sparklers are made using only grapes from that year's harvest. Vintage Champagne or sparkling wine is meant to be an expression of that year rather than the house style. Since these are only made in certain years, vintage sparklers tend to be more expensive.

"I drink champagne when I'm happy and when I'm sad. Sometimes I drink it when I'm alone. When I have company I consider it obligatory. I trifle with it if I'm not hungry and drink it when I am. Otherwise I never touch it - unless I'm thirsty."

~ Madame Lilly Bollinger

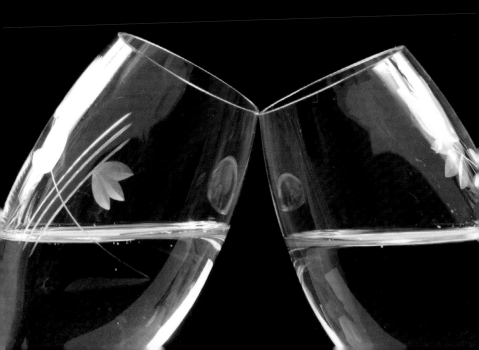

Other Bubblies to Try

Once the sad sisters of Champagne, we now have sparkling wines from France, Spain, Italy and the United States that are just as tasty at a fraction of the cost.

Prosecco. A sparkling wine made in Veneto, a region near Venice, Italy Prosecco is a great way to start any gathering! Fruitier than dry Champagne, this bubbly can appeal to beer drinkers and wine connoisseurs alike. Perfumed, Prosecco can have aromas of apple, citrus honey and wildflowers. Food friendly, it goes with most appetizers, seafood and even spicier dishes. Great Prosecco can be found from $10-$25 a bottle from great producers like Botter, Canella, Mionetto, Zardetto and Carpene Malvolti.

Cava. Made primarily in the Penedès region of northeastern Spain, Cava is often made in the traditional Champagne method. A blend of three grape varieties that are native to Spain, these sparklers can have all the complexity of Champagne. In fact there is more Cava made in the world than any other sparkler! Finer examples are dry and crisp with wonderful citrus flavors and subtle aromas of baked bread. Great with anything you would pair with Champagne or alone! Wonderful

Cavas can be found in many price ranges from under $10 (Freixenet or Cristalino) to pricier bottles (Mont Marçal or Segura Viudas).

> The Bellini was created in 1948 at Harry's Bar in Venice, Italy inspired by an exhibit of the artist Giovan Battista Bellini. It's a mixture of one third white peach nectar and two thirds Prosecco, added to the glass in that order.
> **Feeling ambitious?** Buy some peaches; puree them to create homemade peach nectar.
> **Feeling lazy?** Substitute peach schnapps or buy the pre-mixed Bellinis.

New World sparklers. California (and many other states in the union) make sparkling wines inspired by the greats of Champagne. In many cases, they use the same grapes and processes. Paired with cheeses, oysters and seafood, these bubblies are a great match. Look for brands like Piper Sonoma, Schramsberg, Domaine Chandon, Gruet (NM), Argyle (OR) or Barboursville (VA).

In the bottle. You can find wines that use the production methods developed in Champagne by looking for the terms *méthode champenoise* or *méthode traditionnelle*. The key is that the bubbles are created in the bottle rather than in a tank. Wines made by this method have finer bubbles and more complexity.

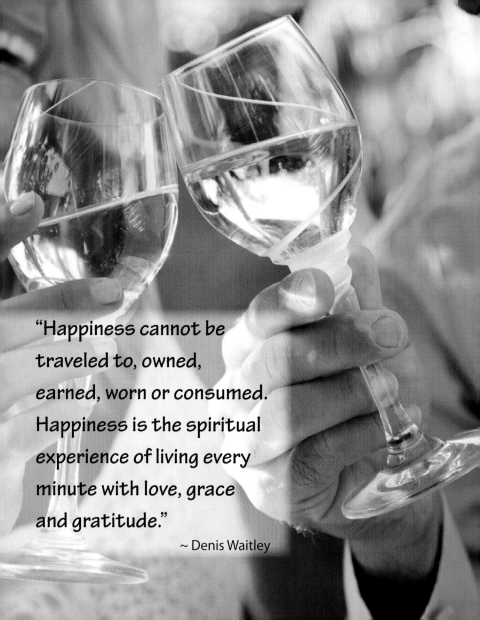

"Happiness cannot be traveled to, owned, earned, worn or consumed. Happiness is the spiritual experience of living every minute with love, grace and gratitude."

~ Denis Waitley

A Toast to Remember

Almost a lost art, a wonderful toast can set the tone of an evening, a friendship, a holiday, or a feast.

Be prepared. Begin your preparation by thinking of what sincerely touches or inspires you about the occasion, guest of honor, or event. What is it that you'd like to express?

Quote a master. Find a great quote that relates to what you'd like to toast (the internet is a great resource). Recite your quote with enthusiasm and end with a hearty "Cheers!"

Short & sweet. Is there anything worse than listening to a rambling speaker while your mouth is as dry as the Sahara? Get to the point, raise your glass, and drink up!

Take a dry run. Even seasoned public speakers rehearse their material. Write out your toast and practice a few times in front of a friend. Write your toast on a note card and bring the note card to the big event to take the pressure off. It's okay to refer to it—just don't read it word for word!

Be you. The best toasts come from the heart via your own humor and style. Don't use a quote or say something that isn't "you."

Safe not sorry! Present your toast early in the evening—many a drunken toast is regretted the next day. Find a toast that is fun yet safe. You don't want to be remembered for a toast that offended or embarrassed others!

Being toasted? As the subject of the toast, you should remain seated if everyone else stands, and sadly, you do not drink. However, afterwards you can stand and thank everyone and then it's bottom's up!

Other Toast Inspiring Quotes:

"My only regret in life is that I did not drink more Champagne."

~John Maynard Keynes, on his deathbed

"Music is the wine that fills the cup of silence."

~Robert Fripp

"May your home always be too small to hold all your friends."

~Old Irish Saying

To Decant or Not to Decant

Ever wonder when or how to use that beautiful decanter on your shelf? Don't worry, you're not alone.

What's the point? There are two main reasons to decant wine. One is to remove the sediment, which is more often found in wines with ten or more years of bottle age and vintage ports. The other reason is to soften young tannic wines through aeration. The astringent or dry finish you get from these youthful reds will soften with decanting.

Into what? Fancy decanters are fun and dramatic to use. But if you don't have a fancy decanter, a glass pitcher or vase can work too. Just make sure that what you pour the wine into is also good for pouring the wine back out.

Get the sed out. To remove sediment from older wines, first, stand the bottle upright for a day or more to allow the sediment to settle to the bottom. Next, remove the entire foil capsule at the top of the bottle and uncork. With the bottle in one hand and the decanter in the other, *slowly* pour the wine into the decanter in a continuous motion. Place a lit candle or flashlight underneath so you can see the wine as it passes through the neck of the bottle. Once you start seeing large grains of sediment, stop pouring! Finally, pour the wine from the decanter into glasses and enjoy!

Airing the youth. To aerate young tannic wine, first, remove the entire foil capsule at the top of the bottle and uncork. Next, pour the wine *vigorously* into the decanter. That's right glug, glug, glug! Let it sit for a few minutes and then pour into glasses. You can also aerate wine by swirling it vigorously in a broad bowl wine glass or pouring from one glass into another and back. This takes longer then using a decanter. But it is fun to take sips in between to taste the evolution of the wine as you continue to aerate it.

The drama. There is, of course, a third reason to decant and that is for the drama! If you've ever been present when a bottle of wine is being decanted in a restaurant, it's difficult not to watch.

"A meal without wine is like a day without sunshine."

~ Anthelme Brillat Savarin

Dessert Wines

How sweet it is! Many of us have forgotten how good a dessert wine can be to top off a meal or evening.

With or as? Dessert wines are sweet and can be served *with* a dessert or *as* the dessert itself to top off a meal. When served *with* a dessert, be sure that the wine is a touch sweeter than the dessert itself (if not, the wine will lose much of its flavor).

Serve 'em up. In general, dessert wines are served in smaller portions than other wines, usually 1-2 ounces. Optimally, they show up in delicate dessert wine glasses, but at home most of us opt for our smaller white wine glasses. Temperature? It depends on the wine. Many dessert wines are best served at 50-60°F. Ice wines should be served a bit colder.

Port. True Port wines, sometimes called *Porto* are fortified wines from Douro region of Portugal. Fortified wines have a neutral grape spirit or brandy added during the winemaking process. For ports, the brandy is added before all the sugar converts to alcohol so there is a bit of sweetness to offset the added strength of the brandy. Port-style wines are also made in Australia, United States and South Africa. There are two main types of port—tawny and ruby. Tawny Ports are known for their dark rich flavors of raisins, toffee, caramel and nuts. These ports are named after their tawny color, which is obtained by aging the wine in oak. Ruby ports are red in color and are not aged in wood. The flavors are more along the lines of red fruits like strawberries as well as plum or apples. Ports are served at the warmer end of the spectrum from 60-65°F.

Sauternes. This area of Bordeaux is known for its legendary sweet wines made mostly the Semillon grape. In order to make this sweet treat, they leave the grapes on the vine until they are affected by a mold. This affliction, affectionately called "noble rot," raisinates the grapes, concentrating their sugars. The winemaker stops the fermentation early in order to leave the right amount of alcohol and sweetness in the wine. These wines go great with fruit based desserts, foie gras and blue cheeses. Sauternes should be served at 50-60°F.

Banyuls. This dessert wine is made from the red grape Grenache in the Rousillon region of southern France. Like port, this wine is fortified before fermentation is complete leaving residual sugar or sweetness. With a rich texture and flavors of raisins, plums, coffee and black cherries, this wine is the perfect partner to chocolate or all by itself! Serve at the same temperature as port.

Ice wine. To make this rare treat, grapes are left on the vine until well into the winter months. During that time they will freeze and thaw several times, concentrating the sugars, acids and flavors. Even though these wines are very sweet, they are perceived drier due to their balancing acidity. The nose of Ice wines includes aromas of peach, mango, fig, honey, lychee, green apple, citrus or pineapple, depending on the grape variety used to make the wine. Look for ice wines from Canada, Germany (where they are called *Eiswein*), Australia, New Zealand and the Unites States. Serve Ice wine on the colder side around 45-50°F.

Moscato d'Asti. Moscato is a semi-sparkling dessert wine made from the Moscato Bianco grape in northwestern Italy in a region called Piedmont. Fizzy and sweet, it is the perfect complement to fruit based desserts, as well as Italian specialties like Zabaglione. Because it has about half the alcohol of most wines, you can afford to have an extra glass! Serve at the same temperature as other sparkling wines at 40-45°F.

"Good wine is a necessity of life for me."

~ Thomas Jefferson

Traditional Holiday Wines

Wines add a special feeling to our traditional holiday fare. Try these as a guide to enhance holiday flavors.

Talking turkey. The rich varied flavors of Thanksgiving respond well to whites like Sauvignon Blanc, Chenin Blanc, dry Riesling, and Viognier. For reds, try Pinot Noir, Shiraz (Syrah) and Zinfandel to create good balance. Beaujolais is also a nice tradition on this holiday.

Sipping with Santa classic. A classic Christmas roast beef in the cold of winter deserves a deep tannic red like a California Cabernet Sauvignon, Bordeaux or even an Italian Barolo. If you are serving ham for your Christmas meal read the suggestions for Easter below.

Ring it in. French Champagne welcomes the New Year elegantly, but Italian Prosecco and Spanish Cava are great choices for a change of pace and to preserve your bank account!

Spring chicks. Serving pork roast or ham for Easter? Try a dry Rosé, Pinot Noir or whites like Riesling and Gewürztraminer as partner for the "other" white meat.

Fireworks. For that casual 4ᵗʰ of July picnic, serve a peppery Shiraz (Syrah) or a jammy Zinfandel for red wine drinkers. For white, consider a Spanish Albariño (pronounced Alba-reen-yo) or an Austrian Grüner Veltliner (pronounced Groo-ner Velt-leener), nicknamed "groovy."

Valentine's Day. For a perfect seductive wine, try a great Rosé Champagne, a spicy Shiraz (Syrah) to heat things up, or some terrific dark chocolate with Port or French Banyuls. Another great chocolate wine is Brachetto d'Acqui. This red semi-sparkling dessert wine is also from the Piedmont region of Italy and has intense raspberry flavors with the perfect amount of sweetness for dark chocolate. Think of it as a raspberry sauce for your chocolate.

President's Day. Thomas Jefferson was one of the biggest supporters of the American wine industry. He felt there was nothing prohibiting America from making great wines like the ones in Europe. Wines from Charlottesville, VA, where he made his home at Monticello, are garnering lots of recognition these days. Look for great Viognier, Merlot or Cabernet Franc from wineries like Blenheim Vineyards (owned by rock star Dave Matthews), Jefferson Vineyards or Barboursville.

"Wine is bottled poetry."

~ Robert Louis Stevenson

Giving the Gift of Wine

Wine is a perfect, thoughtful gift for many occasions. Here are some tips to make sure your offering is welcome:

Always tasteful. From housewarmings to birthdays, French Champagne or nice sparkling wine like Italian Prosecco is always a safe bet. For something a little more unusual, try an Ice Wine or a vintage Port.

Wine Snob? Impress a wine snob by finding unique and unusual grape varietals from more obscure regions, e.g., from Southern Sicily, try Nero D'Avola, from Alsace, opt for Pinot Blanc, from Austria, grab a Grüner Veltliner. Your wine-loving friend will appreciate your thoughtfulness and the new experience.

In the mood. Wine with chocolate is a perfect romantic gesture. Find a Banyuls from Southern France to pair with dark chocolate, or a Brachetto D'Acqui semi-sparkling red dessert wine from Piedmont, Italy.

Wine to dine. Bringing wine to a party or dinner? Choose these crowd pleasers: Sauvignon Blanc, quality Australian Shiraz, an Oregon Pinot Noir, Chardonnay (not too oaky) or Merlot.

Find it fast. If you already know exactly what you want to buy as a gift, try www.winesearcher.com to locate who carries it.

Here are **some** wines that stand the test of time, e.g., to drink at your daughter's graduation or your golden anniversary:

- Vintage Port (Portugal)
- Classified Growth Red Bordeaux (France)
- Grand and Premier Cru Red Burgundy (France)
- Sauternes Dessert Wines (France)
- Barolo and Barbaresco Wines (Piedmont, Italy)
- Tuscan Reds—Brunello di Montalcino, Super Tuscans (Tuscany, Italy)
- High End Cabernet Sauvignon (California, Chile, Australia)

Be sure that the vintage is a good vintage, not an off-year, to ensure it will drink well in years to come.

Great Gifts for Cork Dorks

Wine isn't just a drink, it's an experience! For that truly wine obsessed person on your list choose a gift (other than wine) to enhance their experience.

Glassy eyed. Try special wine glasses they wouldn't buy for themselves, e.g., stemless, dessert/port glasses, outdoors glasses made of acrylic for camping or poolside. Also look at inexpensive, good crystal starter sets for friends just beginning to enjoy wine.

Simply charming. Wine glass charms come in a variety of styles and themes, and are invaluable to know whose glass is whose at lively parties. Got some time? Make them yourself by adding beads and charms to hoop earring forms found at craft stores.

Accessory after the fact. Helpful accessories that wine lovers may not buy for themselves, e.g., wine preserver tools like vacuum stoppers, wine tasting games or kits, attractive decanters, hors d'oeuvres plates with opening for a wine glass, plate clips (allows your wine glass to hang off any plate, freeing your hands), neoprene wine bags that look great and keep wines cool. Though most wine lovers have their own favorite cork screw, an automatic electric cork screw can be fun.

What's that smell? Smell kits are a great way for wine lovers to increase their wine vocabulary. In order to be more specific with your descriptions of the aromas in wine, you need to work your smell muscles. These kits are made with vials of different aromas that you can use alone or at a party to help "remind" your brain of what different fruits, spices, etc. smell like. Later, when you are sniffing your wine, you'll have some idea what you smell.

Have wine, will travel. For those who like to attend outdoor festivals, visit wineries or other wine tasting events, the new accessory to have is a wine neck holder or what I call the "wine necklace." A wine necklace lets you enjoy a hands free experience. Wine necklaces have a comfortable strap to hang any stemmed glass around your neck. They can be found online or at your local wine shop.

"It is well to remember that there are five reasons for drinking; the arrival of a friend; one's present or future thirst; the excellence of the wine; or any other reason."

~ Latin Saying

"Wine stimulates the appetite and enhances food. It promotes conversation and euphoria and can turn a mere meal into a memorable occasion."

~ Derek Cooper

Cooking with Wine: Do's & Don'ts

As W.C. Fields said so brilliantly, "I love to cook with wine. Sometimes I even put it in the food!"

Reveal, don't conceal. The purpose of wine in cooking is to intensify, enhance and accent the flavor and aroma of food, to fortify the flavor of what you are cooking—*not* to conceal it. As with any seasoning used, care should be taken in the amount of wine used. Too little will add insignificant flavor and too much can be overwhelming.

"Cooking" wine? Let's dispel this myth. When cooking with wine, *only* use a wine that you would drink. The wine will impart its flavor to the food. Do you really want the unpleasant flavor of a barely drinkable wine to ruin your Coq au Vin or Beef Bourguignon?

A strong finish. If you are making a wine sauce, there are two key components: 1) use the wine that you are drinking with the dish or at least a wine you would enjoy drinking, and 2) finish the sauce with the wine, and *do not over reduce it*. The wine maker has put in long hours to perfect the complex flavors. The more you reduce, the more you alter those flavors.

Non-alcoholic? When cooking with wine, it's commonly believed that all of the alcohol is cooked off. This is not totally true. Depending on how long you let the wine cook, only about 60% to 95% of the alcohol is cooked off. Alcohol in wine evaporates at 178°F, while water boils at 212°F. If you deglaze a hot pan with wine, more alcohol than water will evaporate at the beginning. The amount of alcohol decreases in proportion to the amount of water, so there will be less alcohol evaporating. Keep this in mind when cooking for someone sensitive to alcohol.

Which? When? How? There are three main uses for wine in cooking: as a marinade ingredient, as a cooking liquid, and as a flavoring in a finished dish. Begin by following recipes that include wine to get a sense of which wines are used in different methods. Then, experiment on your own! Learning to cook with wine will greatly enhance the flavors of many of your favorite dishes. And don't forget to save a glass of wine for the chef!

Quick Grape Guide

Riesling

Pronunciation: rees-ling

Not Just for Dessert. Believe it or not, plenty of wine experts regard quality Rieslings as some of the best wines in the world. Originating in Germany, most are expected to be stereotypically sweet, but in actuality, many Rieslings are dry and crisp. Aromas of apples, pears, peaches and apricots are classic fruit aromas for Riesling. A hint of petroleum along with a steely mineral nose is common for Rieslings.

What to eat with Riesling: A well made dry Riesling is one of the most versatile wines in the world. It will pair well with most dishes, including appetizers, fish, ceviche, chicken, seafood, crab, ham, roasted duck, pork and sushi. The off-dry (or just barely sweet) style Rieslings go well with sushi, spicy Chinese and Thai dishes. Sweeter styles like Auslese and Beerenauslese will be the perfect accompaniment to your fruit based desserts. When it comes to Rieslings there is something for everyone!

Where to find great Rieslings? Some of the best Rieslings are made in Germany, Alsace, New Zealand, Australia, New York (the Finger Lakes region), California and Washington.

If Riesling were a person it would be described as "The Friendliest"
Riesling is at home talking stats with the jocks or solving the world's problems with the book worms. Sometimes it is dry with an edge; other times, soft and super sweet. The Riesling is often misunderstood because people tend to overlook its elegance when dry and only think of this wine's sweet side. Whether sweet or dry, Riesling's crisp acidity allows it to age gracefully.

Sauvignon Blanc
Pronunciation: SOH-veen-yown blanck

The sprite of wine. Sauvignon Blanc, has a zesty personality with vibrant aromas of all things citrus especially grapefruit, green apple, herbs, grass and melon. Its crisp acidity with balancing fruit flavors makes this a popular wine to many especially in the summer months.

What to eat with Sauvignon Blanc: Salads, seafood, fish, chicken, turkey, veal, pork, Asian food, raw oysters and difficult to pair foods like artichokes and crudités. Sauvignon Blanc is one of those rare wines that pairs well with Mexican food. Actually anything you

Looking for German Riesling?
The wine labels can be confusing. To match your specific taste requirements, it is best to know these ripeness levels organized in order of increasing sweetness:

- **Kabinett:** lightest, driest level

- **Spätlese:** a later harvest (riper) style - more body & intensity

- **Auslese:** fuller & sweeter

- **Beerenauslese:** sweet, dessert wine style

- **Trockenbeerenauslese:** richest & sweetest

- **Eiswein:** an ice wine made from concentrated frozen grapes - very concentrated and sweet

squeeze lemon or lime on will go with Sauvignon Blancs including salads and seafood.

Where to find great Sauvignon Blanc? The Loire Valley in France—towns like Sancerre or Pouilly Fumé, South Africa, Chile, California (often labeled as a Fumé Blanc) as well as some of the brightest examples coming from New Zealand. This grape blends particularly well with Semillon, as is the tradition in the whites of Bordeaux.

If Sauvignon Blanc were a person it would be described as "The Girl or Boy Next Door" If nothing else Sauvignon Blanc is high energy, outgoing and refreshing. This grape does well alone or paired with others (especially seafood). Instantly recognizable by its citrus snappiness, it is grown and respected all over the world in places like France, California, New Zealand, Chile and Italy.

Pinot Grigio (a.k.a. Pinot Gris)
Pronunciations: PEE-noh GREE-jee-o or PEE-noh GREE

The grape of many personalities. Pinot Grigio is the white relative of Pinot Noir and can be hard to define since this grape can be blue, white, brown, or even pink, and is made in a variety of styles. Pinot Grigio can be light bodied and crisp or fuller and intense with a hint of spiciness. Either way, you'll experience a crisp white wine full of vibrant citrus fruit (with a hint of floral aromas) making them suitable for pairing with food or sipping solo.

What to eat with Pinot Grigio: The natural acidity found in Italian Pinot Grigio, makes pairing these wines a natural with acidic foods like tomatoes and tomato sauces. Goat cheese, rich pastas, and seafood all make for fantastic marriages with a glass of Pinto Grigio. Those with a fuller body stand up perfectly to pork, chicken, meatier fish, turkey and veal.

Where to find great Pinot Grigio? Pinot Grigio is best known for its homeland Italy where they produce both inexpensive light styles as well as more serious examples found in the northeastern regions of Fruili or Trentino-Alto Adige. Excellent Pinot Gris can be found in Alsace, France and the Willamette Valley of Oregon, Austria, California, New Zealand and Germany (called *Ruländer*).

If Pinot Grigio were a person it would be described as "The Free Spirit" Adaptable to a variety of situations and environments, Pinot Grigio cannot be easily described. Crisp and outgoing when in Italy, full and spicy in Alsace and somewhere in between in Oregon. This grape can do it all! Don't try to pin down this grape, it has a mind of its own!

Chardonnay
Pronunciation: Shahr-dun-NAY

Big, bold, and beautiful. We love our Chardonnay. From wine "newbies" to connoisseurs, Chardonnay tops the list for most Americans. Rich yet delicate, this white grape is made in a plethora of styles from a crisp and steely Chablis to huge oaky versions from California. Used in both still and sparkling wines, Chardonnay is known for its elegance with aromas of citrus, apple, pear and tropical fruits. When aged in oak this variety tends to take on the barrel flavors easily so if it is overdone the oak can dominate the wine. Oak will impart aromas of vanilla, toast, smoke, and coconut.

What to eat with Chardonnay: Because of its unusually dry qualities, Chardonnay goes best with poultry or seafood dishes like lobster and scallops. Some Chardonnays can even be perfectly paired with grilled meat dishes. Looking for a fantastic wine to pair with your favorite cheeses? Chardonnay is a dream paired with milder varieties like Brie and Gruyere.

Where to find great Chardonnay? Chardonnay most likely originated in the Burgundy region of France where some of the most elegant (and expensive) wines are made. These days, vineyards all over the world produce great versions of Chardonnay, including California, Oregon, New Zealand, Australia, Italy, Chile and Argentina.

If Chardonnay were a person it would be described as "Most Popular" Known and loved all over the world, Chardonnay can be elegant and rich, as well as crisp and refreshing. Unfortunately, it is rarely without its partner oak, especially in California. This is a shame since this grape's authentic self is quite impressive.

Pinot Noir (a.k.a. Burgundy)
Pronunciation: PEE-noh nwahr

Food's best friend. One of the most food friendly wines on the planet, this is the grape of obsession. Once you have had an exemplary version of Pinot you will be hooked. Finding great affordable Pinots can be a full time job. Somewhere between super-powered and subtle lives the mighty Pinot Noir. Not as full-bodied and in your face as a Cabernet, or as simple and fruity as a Merlot, a great Pinot Noir is quite frequently—a wine lover's favorite. Pinot is a finicky grape. Conditions must be right for it to show its beauty with complex aromas of cherries, strawberries, raspberries, nutmeg, rose petal, oregano, mushrooms and sometimes violets.

What to eat with Pinot Noir: Soft tannins with balancing acidity make this a versatile match for most any cuisine. Pair your favorite Pinot with poultry, pork, or lamb, mushrooms and oily fishes like tuna and salmon. Trying to convert a white drinker to red? Pinot is an excellent place to start. Ample fruit, soft tannins and its silky smooth texture make this an easy red for white drinkers to love.

Where to find great Pinot Noir? Top regions for the grape include the Burgundy region of France, Willamette Valley in Oregon, New Zealand, Italy (called *Pinot Nero*), Austria, Germany (called *Spätburgunder*), cooler regions of Australia like the Yarra Valley and areas of California, such as Russian River and Monterey.

If Pinot Noir were a person it would be described as "The Diva" Pinot Noir can be thin-skinned and temperamental during youth, but if treated with TLC, it matures into quite a package. Appealing to both red and white drinkers alike, it has all the flavors of red wine, but it is lighter bodied than most reds. It's legendary for its success in Burgundy, in the movie "Sideways" and it has really taken off Down Under!

Merlot
Pronunciation: Mehr-LOW

The user-friendly red. Contrary to the sentiment of the character Miles in the movie "Sideways," Merlot is in many ways the unsung hero of the wine world. It's a great entry variety for newcomers, as it is fruitier and softer than most other reds. Merlot is loaded with flavors, like currant, black cherries, plum, blackberries, blueberries, violets and even a peppery punch. Merlot is one of the best grapes for blending. As an early ripening variety this grape can be used to fill in when other grapes, like Cabernet Sauvignon, do not perform.

What to eat with Merlot: A delicious glass of Merlot fits perfectly with a summery lunch filled with salads topped with berry vinaigrette, light tomato sauce pastas, grilled meats, chicken, pork, tuna, salmon and mildly spiced meat selections. Avoid super spicy dishes, delicate courses or strong cheese like roquefort or gorgonzola.

Where to find great Merlot? Top producing regions include the right bank regions of Bordeaux (St. Emilion and Pomerol), Washington, California (Napa and Sonoma Valleys), Italy, Argentina and Chile. Large volumes of Merlot are produced covering a vast spectrum of quality and price ranges. Some warrant the profanity of Miles, but many do not. Work with your retailer or sommelier to find your favorites.

If Merlot were a person it would be described as "Lovable" Soft, cuddly and fruity, it is hard not to fall in love with a Merlot. When it is treated right it can be the perfect wine for a party, to relax after work or for your backyard cookouts. If overproduced and not treated with care your love for Merlot can easily turn to disdain.

Syrah (a.k.a. Shiraz)
Pronunciations: See-RAH or SHEAR-oz

As spicy as it wants to be. The Syrah grape is a bold, spicy little number that can provide a memorable wine experience. Deep purple in color it produces medium to full-bodied wines. Syrah typically possesses firm tannins, ripe and smooth in nature, as opposed to abrasive varieties from younger reds. Depending on its origins some of the most notable flavors from Syrah include blackberry, black currant, black peppers, clove, licorice, dark chocolate and bacon. Complex? You bet!

What to eat with Syrah: Syrah is a match made in heaven when paired with grilled meats, stews and barbeque dishes. This bold red can stand up to the gamiest, richest of proteins. Don't feel like cooking? Order a pizza and pour a glass of Shiraz for the perfect night in.

Where to find great Syrah? The most prominent regions for making a mean Syrah are the Northern Rhône region of France, the Barossa and Hunter Valleys in Australia, South Africa, Chile, and Argentina. For domestic Syrah, consider California, Washington and parts of Oregon.

If Syrah were a person it would be described as "Life of the Party" With its classic peppery aromas, Syrah really knows how to spice things up! A bit of a chameleon, Syrah can be the lighter "live for today" type, or a more serious, age worthy character. This varietal is loved by party goers in many countries including Australia, California, and South Africa.

Cabernet Sauvignon

Pronunciation: Cah-burr-NAY Sow-vee-NYOH

All Hail the King. If grapes were royalty Cabernet Sauvignon would most certainly reign as king. Cab, as it is nicknamed, is immensely popular, age worthy and one of the major ingredients in the heralded wines of Bordeaux. Known for its full body, firm tannins and bold flavors this is one grape that you can't ignore. Cabernet tends to have a variety of black fruit aromas like blackberry, black currant, plum and black cherry along with rosemary, bell pepper, mint, eucalyptus, tea, cedar as well as oak influence. Depending on its origin, earthy aromas like mushroom, tobacco, mineral, leather or tar may also be present.

What to eat with Cabernet Sauvignon: Remember three things in pairing with Cabs—Bold, Grilled and Fat. Cabernet matches well with bolder foods that match its intensity especially grilled meats. Fats found in meat and cream sauces will naturally tame the astringent tannins found in Cabernets. Avoid delicate dishes that will pale in comparison to this hearty red.

Where to find great Cabernet Sauvignon? Bordeaux continues to be the region most associated with the production of Cabernet

Sauvignon, but other parts of the world have mastered the art as well. Napa and Sonoma Valleys have earned respect for their top notch Cabs, as have Chile, Argentina, South Africa, and Australia. Tuscany's sought after "Super Tuscans" often use Cabernet to achieve their greatness. Other regions where Cab can thrive include Walla, Walla, Washington, the Hawkes Bay region of New Zealand and the north fork of Long Island.

If Cabernet Sauvignon were a person it would be described as "The Powerhouse" You know the type—big, bold and in your face. Cabernet is handsome, well respected, but can be aggressive in its youth, but it gets softer and more approachable with age. Its success in Bordeaux, California and Australia has made this one of the most revered grapes in the world—over time it will outlast them all.

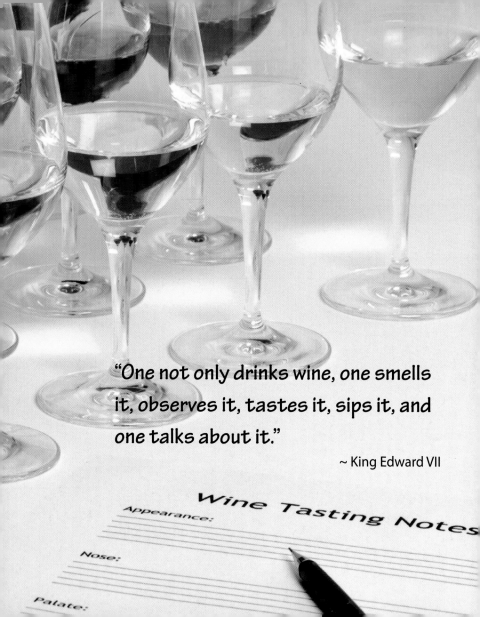

"One not only drinks wine, one smells it, observes it, tastes it, sips it, and one talks about it."

~ King Edward VII

Wine Tasting Notes

Appearance:

Nose:

Palate:

It's No Fun to Drink Alone!

Starting a wine club with friends is a fun and economical way to taste your way to becoming wine savvy. You'll be surprised how much more you have to discuss while you're tasting wine!

Here are the key steps to beginning your wine club:

Choose your team wisely. In order to have a fun and successful club, pick friends and acquaintances who love wine as much as you do (or at least have the desire to learn). The ideal group is 6-12 core members where one person (possibly you) takes the role as the group's leader. Another consideration is budget. Each month, members will contribute to offset the costs of the wine. It is crucial that all members are committed to making that investment. The good news is that pooling your financial resources means you can taste many more wines than you could afford to sample alone.

Create a name and mission for your group. At the first organizational meeting, have a celebratory glass of bubbly and brainstorm for creative names for the group. This can be lots of fun and a way to break the ice if some members are meeting each other for the first time. A flip chart and lots of colored markers or a steno pad can be used to record the best ideas. Are you the *Silver Sippers* or possibly the *Merlot Mamas*? It's up to you! It is also good to decide on your mission. Is the goal to try some great wines and socialize? Or is it to expand your wine knowledge? To avoid issues later, it is important that everyone starts out with the same expectations.

Create a calendar of tastings for the coming year. Everyone should sign up to host one of the monthly meetings. The host is responsible for purchasing the wines within the agreed-upon budget. It probably makes sense to focus on wines within the $15-$40 range since that is where most people are comfortable. For the first meeting, invite a wine educator, sommelier or owner of your favorite wine store to instruct the group on the elements of tasting. In subsequent months, the host commits to doing a bit of research that s/he shares with the group about the wines and their region. Invest in a wine reference like *Oxford Companion to Wine* by Jancis Robinson so your group can look up unfamiliar terms or concepts.

Develop your wine source. Since the group will be buying a good deal of wine over the coming year, find a wine store to support you. A store with a great variety of wines in all price ranges is crucial. Many stores have sales associates who are either certified wine professionals or avid wine enthusiasts who can be a great asset in selecting your wines. Store owners and sales people typically taste 30 or more wines each week, so they are a wealth of "tasting" knowledge. Who knows, they may even want to join your club! Ask if they offer any discounts or materials to support your wine club in exchange for making them your "club" approved store.

Conduct the kickoff tasting! Key essentials needed at each meeting are wine glasses, spit or dump buckets, water to stay hydrated, and a way for members to record their observations of each wine. Each member brings an appetizer to be enjoyed after all wines are sampled. It is often helpful to limit the tastings to four to six wines and taste them blind. Blind tasting means the identity of each wine is kept hidden until all wines are sampled. This way members focus on the wine itself, keeping preconceived notions from swaying members' opinions. You can buy a set of wine bags, use aluminum foil or just use brown paper bags to cover up the bottles. The host leads the group through the tasting, and after all wines are tasted, the wines are unveiled and the discussions can begin! It is important that everyone feels comfortable to share their preferences without being judged. As it is with art or food, taste in wine can be very subjective. No one is right or wrong.

Keep a wine journal and take pictures. Each member would be wise to keep a wine notebook or journal to record thoughts and preferences at each tasting. Make sure to note some good descriptors on the aromas/flavors of the wine as well as your overall impression of the wine. Make a star next to wines you really like and would want to purchase again. A simple tasting process to use for your meetings is shown in the box below.

For a useful format to record your wine notes see page 119, to download *visit:* www.thewinecoach.com/thesippingpoint

Another trick to remember all that you taste is to take a picture of each bottle's label. Take pictures not just of labels to record everyone having fun. Email members the invitation for the next month's meeting with a link to your pictures. That is a sure way to keep them coming back!

Here's some great themes for your wine club meetings:

- The Big Six Tasting – Riesling, Sauvignon Blanc, Chardonnay, Pinot Noir, Merlot and Cabernet
- ABC: Anything but Chardonnay or Cabernet
- Wines You Can't Pronounce
- Spanish Reds under $20
- Forget Basket Bottoms: The New Chianti
- Italian Pinot Grigio vs. Oregon Pinto Gris
- Oregon Pinot Noir vs. French Burgundy
- A Groovy Tasting: Grüner Veltliners from Austria
- Syrah from All over the World
- Australian Shiraz
- Think Pink with Rosés
- Champagne: The Real Stuff
- Bubbly 101: Sparklers from around the World
- Ice Wine Tasting
- Rebels without a Cork®: Screw Cap Wines
- Pretty as a Picture: Wines with Great Labels

"One barrel of wine can work more miracles than a church full of saints."

~ Old Italian Proverb

Tasting Notes Format

Wine Tasted _____ Vintage_____

Origin _____

Who you tasted it with: _____

Look

–White: ❐ Green   ❐ Yellow   ❐ Straw   ❐ Gold   ❐ Amber

–Red: ❐ Purple   ❐ Ruby Red ❐ Brick   ❐ Amber

Smell (list all aromas you recognize)

Taste

Body: ❐ Light   ❐ Medium   ❐ Full

Acidity or the Pucker Factor: ❐ Flabby   ❐ Moderate   ❐ Crisp

Tannin (for reds): ❐ Soft   ❐ Moderate   ❐ Firm, tannic

Describe

Decide

About Laurie Forster

The Wine Coach®

After a successful career in software sales, Laurie decided she was ready for a life change. Through working with a life coach, Laurie began to realize that her biggest passions—wine and people—could be parlayed into a new career. In 2002, she began her wine career in Manhattan where she studied with the American Sommelier Association to obtain her certificate in Viticulture and Vinification. Laurie also trained at the Culinary Institute of America in Napa Valley and later became a member of the Society of Wine Educators.

Concurrently, she trained as a life coach with Coach U, the leading global provider of coach training programs and is presently a member of the International Coaching Federation. Laurie is also dedicated to furthering her learning about wine by going to its source. She's a worldly wine professional whose extensive travels include visiting wineries and vineyards in Australia, New Zealand, Italy, California, Maryland, Virginia, Oregon and New York.

As The Wine Coach®, Laurie creates unique corporate team building events, group tasting seminars and culinary tours. She is dedicated to demystifying wine—one glass at a time, helping build successful teams as well as ensuring that everyone has an inspiring time at her events. Her seminars introduce would-be oenophiles to the enchanting world of wine, while inspiring them to explore their own personal development goals, passions and purpose. She's a sparkling presenter, highly skilled at engaging every wine lover—from beginners to wine enthusiasts.

Laurie is a regular contributor to What's Up Annapolis Magazine, Grapevine Magazine, Business Woman PA and other fine publications. She is a sought after guest expert on radio stations across the country and her weekly radio show "Something to Wine About®" can be heard on WCEI 96.7 FM and WBAL 1090 AM. Laurie is also serving as national spokesperson for the "Pour on The Joy" campaign sponsored by Lindemans® Wines where she is helping people increase their happiness by making the wine-joy connection.

"*Ever get perplexed by a wine list, befuddled by the litany of bottles on the shelves? What goes well with meat? With fish? With cheese? Are you a red person or a white person or both? Not to fear. Thought the world of wine is huge and confusing, Laurie Forster is here to help. . . .*"

~ Carroll County Times, January 11, 2007

"*If you can't pronounce it, order it. These are words to live by, according to Laurie Forster, known throughout Maryland as The Wine Coach.*"

~Baltimore Examiner, March 3, 2008

Laurie Forster, The Wine Coach®
Contact Info: 410-820-4212
Email: laurie@thewinecoach.com
Web: www.TheWineCoach.com

"My recipe for success
is one part wine
education, one part
social interaction,
minus the snooty
attitude. Swirl . . .
Delicious every time!"

~ Laurie Forster, The Wine Coach®

Paragon Light Photography

Want to Schedule a Wine Event or Tour?

Wine Tastings are the new "golf outing" and it's much easier to learn than golf!

Are you tired of looking for the "right" speaker for your next event or conference? Don't all those speakers at the National Speakers Association start to sound alike? If you really want to inspire and impress all your attendees, call on The Wine Coach®!

Whether you're seeking an entertaining way to motivate your sales staff or looking for an innovative way to conduct corporate team building, The Wine Coach® can help!

Laurie Forster, The Wine Coach®, combines her training as a professional sommelier and life coach to create unique events for corporate and private groups. Laurie brings her lively personality and casual, yet informative style to each event she conducts.

The Wine Coach® has made it her mission to demystify wine, one glass at a time. She focuses on creating connections between participants while delivering her unique brand of attitude-free wine education.

The old proverb stating "Over a bottle of wine, many a friend is made" is experienced time and time again at her events.

Let The Wine Coach® events create added value for your:

✔ Conference

✔ Sales meeting

✔ Customer dinner

✔ Incentive travel

✔ Association Meeting

✔ Weekend Retreat

✔ Or just for fun!

Benefits gained from a wine event or incentive trip with The Wine Coach® include:

✔ Wine savvy employees entertaining clients on a budget

✔ Increased morale

✔ Improved teamwork

✔ Stronger relationships with key customers

✔ An experience no one will forget!

Past clients include Merrill Lynch, Met Life, JP Morgan, Lighthouse Marketing, United States Chamber of Commerce, Bovis Lend Lease, Clark Construction, Ritz Carlton Residences, American Business Women's Association, and others.

What do customers say about The Wine Coach®?

"Laurie, The Wine Coach® did a great job creating an enjoyable wine dinner for our clients. She was able to convey to all of our clients something new about wine, even those that are more experienced wine drinkers. She has a very fun and lighthearted approach in talking about wines which made the evening much more interesting than just a simple dinner with our best clients."

~Valerie Campbell
Assistant Vice President,
Merrill Lynch

"Thanks again for the home run experience yesterday! In this morning's debrief on yesterday's learning, there was 'beaucoup' energy on the wine experience. The memorable learning of jelly beans and walnuts, coupled with the utility of words to describe an experience that enhances communication/learning were but two of the many takeaways!"

~Rick Corcoran
RJ Corcoran & Associates LLC,
consultant to the United States
Chamber of Commerce

Contact The Wine Coach®
Call: 410-820-4212
Email: laurie@thewinecoach.com
Web: www.TheWineCoach.com

Do You Want to Know How to Crack open that Wine List & Break the Code to Find Great Tasting Wines that Won't Blow Your Budget?

Have you ever had to plan a wine dinner for friends, family or for work? Have you found it a daunting and stressful task? Let's face it there are thousands of wines to choose from at every price range. It's stressful to ensure that the food is spectacular and to select a wine that pairs perfectly with everyone's meal! Do you feel truly equipped to do this?

Forget all of your worries right now and go to my website to download a copy of my FREE REPORT on Cracking the Code of Wine Lists ($29 Value):

www.TheWineCoach.com/thesippingpoint